The Space Between

Asher Everett

Published by Golden Leaf Haven Publishing, 2024.

Table of Contents

About The Author

Asher Everett is a poet and writer who has always been drawn to the spaces between. Born and raised in the Pacific Northwest, Asher grew up surrounded by the rugged beauty of nature, which instilled in him a deep sense of wonder and awe. This sense of wonder has stayed with him throughout his life, and has become a hallmark of his writing.

Asher's poetry is a reflection of his own journey into the unknown, a voyage through the uncharted territories of the human heart. His words are infused with a sense of longing and searching, as he explores the complexities of love, loss, identity, and belonging. With a unique voice and a keen eye for observation, Asher's poetry is both deeply personal and universally relatable.

Asher's writing has been influenced by a wide range of poets and writers, from the classic works of Walt Whitman and Emily Dickinson to the contemporary voices of Mary Oliver and Warsan Shire. He is also drawn to the works of philosophers and thinkers, such as Rainer Maria Rilke and bell hooks, who have shaped his understanding of the world and his place in it.

When he is not writing, Asher can be found exploring the outdoors, practicing yoga, or simply sitting in silence, listening to the whispers of the universe. He currently resides in a small town in the mountains, where he is working on his next collection of poetry and living a simple, intentional life.

"The Space Between" is Asher's debut poetry collection, and it represents a major milestone in his writing journey. The book is a culmination of years of writing, reflection, and exploration, and it offers a unique glimpse into the mind and heart of this emerging poet. With its release, Asher hopes to connect with readers and inspire them to explore their own spaces between, to listen to their own whispers, and to find their own sense of wonder and awe.

Preface

In the quiet hours of the night, when the world is hushed and the stars shine bright, I find myself drawn to the spaces between. The spaces between words, between breaths, between moments. It is here, in these liminal territories, that I have discovered the true power of poetry.

For me, poetry has always been a journey into the unknown, a voyage through the uncharted territories of the human heart. It is a way of navigating the complexities of love, loss, identity, and belonging; of exploring the depths of our own souls; and of finding meaning in the silence.

This collection, "The Space Between", is a reflection of that journey. It is a gathering of poems that have emerged from the spaces between, poems that have been shaped by the silences, the pauses, and the moments of stillness. They are poems about the human condition, about the fragility and beauty of life, and about the resilience of the human spirit.

As I wrote these poems, I found myself drawn to the threshold between light and darkness, between hope and despair, and between the known and the unknown. I found myself exploring the spaces between the lines, the gaps between the words, and the silences between the breaths. And it is here, in these spaces, that I discovered the true beauty of poetry.

In "The Space Between", I invite you to join me on this journey into the unknown. Let us explore the spaces between together, and let us discover the beauty, the wonder, and the magic that lies within. Let us find the words that speak to our souls, the rhythms that resonate with our hearts, and the silences that echo with our deepest longings.

For in the end, it is not the words that matter, but the spaces between them. It is not the poetry, but the silence that surrounds it. It is not the language, but the longing that it expresses. And it is not the poet, but the reader who brings the words to life.

So let us embark on this journey together, into the space between. Let us find the beauty, the wonder, and the magic that lies within. And let us discover, in the words of the poet, the silence that speaks to our souls.

Asher Everett
25th March, 2024

Stare

I lose myself in the depths of your eyes
A universe of wonder, a sea of surprise
The world outside fades, and I am drawn in
To the mystery, the magic, the beauty within

My gaze is held captive, my soul on fire
As I stare into the abyss, and the abyss stares back at me, higher
The silence is palpable, the tension is real
As I search for answers, and the truth begins to reveal

In the stillness, I find a sense of peace
A sense of calm, a sense of release
The world may be chaotic, but in this moment, I am free
To stare, to gaze, to lose myself in the beauty of thee

The minutes tick by, the hours slip away
As I stand frozen, lost in the depths of your gaze
The world outside recedes, and I am left alone
To stare, to ponder, to make sense of the unknown

In the darkness, I find a sense of light
A sense of hope, a sense of what's right
The stars align, the planets converge
As I stare into the void, and the void stares back at me, emerge

So let me stare, let me gaze
Let me lose myself in the depths of your eyes, in the beauty of your face
For in the stillness, I find a sense of peace
A sense of calm, a sense of release.

In The Sand

I stand on the shore, where the waves meet the land
The sand beneath my feet, a shifting, shifting sand
The tide rises high, the tide falls low
Leaving behind a trail, of secrets, yet to be known

I walk along the beach, where the sun meets the sea
The sand warm between my toes, a feeling of serenity
The wind whispers secrets, of the depths below
As I search for treasures, in the sand, where the waves do flow

In the sand, I find a shell, a fragment of a tale
A story of the ocean, of the waves that never fail
To erode, to shape, to mold and to form
The sand, the shore, the landscape, in a constant storm

I dig my hands into the sand, feeling the grains slip away
Like the moments of my life, like the hours, the days
The sand is fleeting, ephemeral, a temporary hold
On the memories, the emotions, the stories, yet to be told

In the sand, I find a peace, a sense of calm and rest
A feeling of connection, to the earth, to the best
The sand, the sea, the sky, a symphony of sound
A reminder of the beauty, that's always to be found

As the sun sets over the sea, casting a golden glow
I stand in the sand, feeling the warmth, the light, the flow
Of the universe, of life, of the moments, yet to come
In the sand, I find a sense of home, a sense of being, a sense of being one.

The sand, it holds my footprints, a temporary mark
A reminder of my presence, a sign of my embark
On the journey of life, on the path, I've yet to roam
In the sand, I find a sense of freedom, a sense of being, a sense of being
home.

Born Like This

I was born with a heart that beats
To the rhythm of a different drum, it repeats
A melody that's unique, a harmony that's mine
A symphony that echoes, a refrain that's divine

My soul was forged in fire, my spirit was refined
In the crucible of life, I was tempered and aligned
To the frequencies of love, to the vibrations of light
I was born to shine, to radiate, to ignite

I was born with a voice that speaks
A language that's authentic, a tone that's unique
A dialect that's raw, a vocabulary that's real
A message that's honest, a truth that I feel

My eyes were opened wide, my mind was expanded
To the possibilities, to the potential, to the promised land
I was born to explore, to discover, to create
To bring forth new worlds, to innovate, to participate

I was born like this, with a heart that's wild
A spirit that's free, a soul that's undefiled
I was born to roam, to wander, to stray
To follow my path, to find my way

I was born like this, with a voice that's clear
A message that's strong, a truth that's dear
I was born to speak, to shout, to sing
To make my presence known, to take my rightful ring

I was born like this, with a heart that's full
A spirit that's fierce, a soul that's unbroken and unfulled
I was born to live, to love, to laugh, to cry
To feel the depth, to touch the sky

So let me be, let me breathe
Let me live my truth, let me be me
I was born like this, and I won't apologize
For being different, for being unique, for being alive.

Chronic

My body is a battlefield, a war zone in my skin
A constant barrage of pain, a relentless attack within
The enemy is invisible, a silent and stealthy foe
A chronic condition, a lifelong sentence to endure and know

The days blend together, a never-ending haze
Of fatigue and fog, of pain and daze
The nights are long and sleepless, a restless and fitful sleep
As my body protests and rebels, its cries and screams I must keep

The medications and treatments, a cocktail of chemicals and art
A delicate balance of dosages, a fragile and fragile heart
The side effects and symptoms, a laundry list of woes
A constant juggling act, as I try to find some reprieve and some repose

But still I rise, still I face the day
With a determination and a courage, that I never knew I'd sway
I adapt and I adjust, I find new ways to cope
I learn to live with the chronic, to find a new sense of hope

For even in the darkness, there is a light that shines
A beacon of resilience, a flame that flickers and divine
A reminder that I am strong, that I am capable and brave
A chronic condition, but not a definition, not a wave

I am more than my illness, more than my pain
I am a warrior, a fighter, a survivor, a soul that remains
Unbroken and unbowed, I stand and I face the test
A chronic condition, but not a defeat, not a rest

So I'll rise up and I'll fight, I'll take on the day
With a spirit that's unbroken, with a heart that's still at play
I'll find a way to thrive, to live and to love and to be
A chronic condition, but not a limitation, not a destiny.

Burn

My heart is a flame, a fire that burns so bright
A passion that consumes me, a love that ignites
The fuel that feeds the fire, a desire that never fades
A burning need to create, to express, to convey

The embers glow with intensity, a heat that never subsides
A burning ambition, a drive that never divides
The flames that flicker and dance, a rhythm that never grows old
A burning passion that guides me, a fire that never grows cold

In the darkness, the fire burns, a beacon in the night
A guiding light that shines so bright, a burning sense of right
The flames that rise and fall, a symphony of sound
A burning melody that echoes, a harmony that's found

The fire that burns within me, a flame that never dies
A burning sense of purpose, a passion that never compromises
The heat that radiates from me, a warmth that never fades
A burning love that shines so bright, a flame that's never jaded

But like all fires, it can burn, it can rage and it can roar
A burning fury that consumes, a passion that can't be ignored
The flames that lick and flicker, a danger that's always near
A burning reminder of the power, of the fire that I hold dear

So I'll tend the flames with care, I'll feed the fire with might
I'll let it burn and rage and roar, through the dark of night
For in the fire, I find my strength, my passion and my voice
A burning sense of purpose, a flame that makes my heart rejoice

The burn of the fire, it never fades, it never grows old
A burning sense of wonder, a flame that never grows cold
It's the fire that drives me, the passion that ignites
A burning sense of purpose, a flame that shines so bright.

Just Like You

I see the way you smile, the way you laugh and play
The way you light up the room, and brighten up the day
I see the way you care, the way you love and give
And I am drawn to you, like a magnet, I want to live

Just like you, I want to shine, to radiate love and light
To be a beacon in the darkness, a guiding star in the night
Just like you, I want to be, a source of hope and peace
A refuge from the storm, a safe and gentle release

I see the way you move, the way you walk and talk
The way you carry yourself, with confidence and a gentle chalk
I see the way you connect, the way you touch and feel
And I am inspired by you, to be more real

Just like you, I want to be, authentic and true
To let my guard down, and let my heart shine through
Just like you, I want to love, with abandon and with glee
To give myself fully, and let my spirit be free

We may be different, in shape and size and hue
But deep down, we're the same, with hearts that beat and feel anew
We all have hopes and dreams, we all have fears and doubts
But with you, I feel a sense of kinship, a sense of being without

Just like you, I am imperfect, I am flawed and I am weak
But with you, I feel a sense of strength, a sense of being unique
Just like you, I am a work of art, a masterpiece in the making
A beautiful and intricate tapestry, with threads of love and heart that's
breaking

So let's be just like each other, let's shine our lights so bright
Let's be a reflection of love, a beacon in the dark of night
Let's be a source of hope and peace, a refuge from the storm
Just like you, I want to be in a beautiful and gentle form.

Home

My heart is a wanderer, a traveler of the soul
It roams the world, searching for a place to call its own
It's been to distant lands, and seen the beauty of the earth
But no matter where it goes, it's always searching for its birth

Home is a feeling, a sense of belonging and peace
A place where the heart can rest, and the soul can release
It's a place where love resides, where memories are made
A place where the heart can heal, and the soul can be remade

I've been to many places, and seen the beauty of the land
But none of them have felt like home, none of them have felt like my stand
I've walked the streets of cities, and felt the rush of the crowd
But none of them have felt like home, none of them have felt like my cloud

But then I saw your face, and felt my heart skip a beat
I saw the love in your eyes, and felt my soul find its seat
I felt a sense of belonging, a sense of being home
I felt like I had found my place, my heart's sweet roam

You are my home, my safe and peaceful place
My heart's refuge, my soul's escape
You are my haven, my shelter from the storm
My heart's forever home, my love, my form

In your arms, I find my peace, my heart's sweet release
In your love, I find my home, my soul's forever ease
You are my home, my heart's forever stand
My love, my heart, my home, my everything, my hand

So let me stay with you, let me rest in your love
Let me call you home, my heart, my soul, my everything above
For with you, I am home, I am free, I am me
With you, my love, I am home, wild and carefree.

Scared

My heart is racing, my soul is on fire
I'm trapped in a nightmare, and I don't know how to retire
The fears that haunt me, the doubts that creep
They whisper my name, and make my heart leap

I'm scared of the darkness, of the unknown and the night
I'm scared of being alone, of being without a light
I'm scared of being hurt, of being broken and worn
I'm scared of being lost, of being forever forlorn

I'm scared of my own voice, of the words that I speak
I'm scared of being heard, of being seen and unique
I'm scared of being rejected, of being turned away
I'm scared of being loved, of being loved in a way that's not okay

I'm scared of the future, of the unknown and the unseen
I'm scared of the past, of the memories that still linger and gleam
I'm scared of the present, of the moment that's here and now
I'm scared of being stuck, of being frozen in a moment that won't allow

But most of all, I'm scared of myself
Of the thoughts that I think, of the feelings that I feel and wealth
I'm scared of my own power, of the strength that I possess
I'm scared of my own weakness, of the vulnerabilities that I repress

So I'll hide behind my fears, and let them control my mind
I'll let them whisper lies, and make me leave my heart behind
I'll let them hold me back, and keep me from being free
I'll let them scare me, and make me believe that I'm not me

But then I'll remember, that I am strong and brave
That I can face my fears, and let my heart be saved
I'll remember that I'm not alone, that I have a voice and a choice
I'll remember that I can rise, and let my spirit rejoice

So I'll stand up to my fears, and let them know that I'm not afraid
I'll face them head-on, and let my heart be displayed
I'll let my voice be heard, and let my spirit shine
I'll be scared, but I'll be brave, and I'll make it through the night.

Let You Down

I'm sorry for the times I've let you down
For the promises I've broken, and the love I've worn out
I'm sorry for the tears I've caused, and the pain I've brought
For the moments I've missed, and the memories I've forgot

I know I've failed you, in so many ways
I've fallen short of your expectations, and faded away
I've let my doubts and fears, get the best of me
And I've let you down, in the process, repeatedly

I remember the nights, you stayed up late
Waiting for me to come home, and ease your troubled state
But I didn't show up, and I didn't call
I left you hanging, and I let you fall

I know I've hurt you, and I'm truly sorry
For the times I've let you down, and made you feel like you're not worthy
I'm sorry for the times, I've made you feel alone
And for the moments, I've let my own fears, take control

But I want you to know, that I'm trying to be strong
I'm trying to be the one, you can count on, all day long
I'm trying to be the rock, that you can lean on
And I'm trying to be the safe haven, where you can call home

I know it won't be easy, and it won't be fast
But I promise to work hard, to regain your trust at last
I'll do everything in my power, to make it right
And I'll spend the rest of my life, making sure you feel my love and light

So please don't give up on me, don't lose your faith
I'll do everything I can, to make sure you're not let down again, in this
life
I'll be there for you, through the ups and downs
And I'll do my best, to turn it around, and make it right, in this town

I'll let you down, no more, I swear it's true
I'll be the one you can count on, and I'll see it through
I'll be your rock, your safe haven, your guiding light
And I'll make sure you know that you're loved, and you're not alone, in
this fight.

Now Or Never

The clock is ticking, the moment's here
A choice to make, a decision to clear
The path ahead, a fork in the road
To take the leap, or to let it go

Now or never, the time is right
To seize the day, and make it shine so bright
To take the chance, and make it real
To make the move, and let the heart feel

The fear of failure, it whispers low
Of doubts and worries, that only grow
But the heart beats strong, with a desire to try
To take the risk, and reach for the sky

Now or never, the moment's mine
To take the step, and make it all mine
To let go of fear, and let love shine
To make the choice, and make it all divine

The future's uncertain, the outcome unknown
But the present moment, it's all my own
To take the leap, and make it happen now
To seize the day, and let my spirit vow

Now or never, the time is here
To make the move, and wipe away the tear
To take the chance, and make it real
To make the choice, and let my heart feel

The world is waiting, with all its might
For me to take the leap, and make it shine so bright
The moment's mine, the choice is clear
To take the step, and banish all fear

Now or never, the time is now
To make the move, and let my spirit vow
To take the leap, and make it happen now
To seize the day, and let my heart shine somehow.

Drown

I'm sinking deep, into the dark and cold
The water's rising, and I'm growing old
I'm trying to breathe, but it's hard to stay
Afloat in the ocean, where the waves crash and sway

I'm drowning in my thoughts, in the sea of my mind
The emotions are overwhelming, and I'm losing my grip in time
I'm searching for a lifeline, a rope to cling to tight
But it's slipping away, and I'm sinking into the night

The weight is crushing me, the pressure's getting strong
I'm trying to escape, but I'm stuck in this song
The melody is haunting, the rhythm is slow
I'm drowning in the silence, where the music used to flow

I'm lost in the depths, of my own despair
The darkness is surrounding me, and I don't know how to repair
The damage is done, the hurt is real
I'm drowning in my tears, and I don't know how to feel

But then I see a light, a glimmer in the dark
A beacon of hope, a shining spark
It's calling me to rise, to break the surface tension
To find my way back, to the world's intention

I'm swimming to the top, with all my might
I'm fighting to stay alive, to shine with all my light
I'm breaking through the waves, and I'm feeling alive
I'm rising above the pain, and I'm starting to thrive

I won't let the water, take me down to the sea
I won't let the darkness, consume me completely
I'll find my way to shore, I'll rise above the tide
I'll learn to breathe again, and I'll survive to live and thrive.

Wake Up

The alarm is ringing, the morning light is bright
A new day is dawning, and it's time to take flight
The world is waking up, and it's time to rise
To shake off the slumber, and open your eyes

The darkness of night, is fading away
As the sun rises high, and a new day is born to stay
The stars are disappearing, as the light takes its place
And the world is waking up, with a smile on its face

Wake up, wake up, it's time to begin
A new day is waiting, and it's time to take a step within
The possibilities are endless, the opportunities are wide
Wake up, wake up, and let your spirit glide

The morning dew is glistening, the birds are singing their song
The world is coming alive, and it's time to move along
The coffee is brewing, the day is young and fresh
Wake up, wake up, and let your heart be refreshed

Wake up, wake up, and let your dreams unfold
A new day is waiting, and it's time to take control
The future is uncertain, but one thing is clear
Wake up, wake up, and let your spirit persevere

The world needs your presence, your voice and your light
Wake up, wake up, and let your beauty shine so bright
The morning is a gift, a new beginning every day
Wake up, wake up, and let your heart find its way

So rise and shine, and let the morning sun shine bright
Wake up, wake up, and let your spirit take flight
The world is waiting for you, with all its might
Wake up, wake up, and let your heart ignite.

Take Me Under

The waves are calling, the tide is high
I'm standing on the edge, feeling the ocean's sigh
The water's whispering, a soothing melody
Take me under, and set my soul free

The world above is loud, it's chaotic and bright
But in the depths below, I'll find my peaceful night
The pressure's intense, the darkness is complete
But in the silence, I'll find my heart's retreat

Take me under, where the light can't shine
Where the noise of the world, is just a distant hum and whine
I'll let the water's weight, press down on me
And in the stillness, I'll find my ecstasy

The ocean's vast and wide, it's mysterious and deep
A world of wonder, where my spirit can creep
The creatures of the sea, they'll be my guide
As I explore the depths, where the unknown resides

Take me under, where the currents are strong
Where the waves will carry me, to a place where I belong
I'll let the water's power, sweep me away
And in the undertow, I'll find my own way

In the darkness of the deep, I'll find my light
A glowing ember, that will guide me through the night
The ocean's secrets, they'll be mine to keep
As I surrender to the waves, and let my spirit sleep

Take me under, and I'll be reborn
In the depths of the ocean, where my heart will be transformed
I'll emerge anew, with a soul that's refreshed and bright
And in the world above, I'll shine with a newfound light.

It's All Over

The final curtain call, the last goodbye
The end of an era, the closing of an eye
The flame that once burned bright, has flickered out of sight
It's all over, and the darkness takes its night

The memories linger, like a ghost in my mind
A bittersweet reminder, of what we left behind
The laughter, the tears, the joy and the pain
All echoes of a love, that will never be the same

The silence is deafening, the stillness is cold
The emptiness is overwhelming, the heart is old
The fire that once warmed, has reduced to ashes and grey
It's all over, and the winter of our love has come to stay

I'm left to pick up the pieces, of a heart that's broken and worn
To try and make sense of it all, and find a way to move on
But it's hard to let go, when the memories still remain
Of the love we had, and the love that we couldn't sustain

It's all over, and I'm left to face the night
Alone and adrift, without your loving light
The stars are shining bright, but they offer no comfort or peace
For in their twinkling beauty, I'm reminded of your release

The world keeps spinning, the sun keeps shining bright
But for me, it's all over, and the darkness takes its night
I'll wander through the shadows, trying to find my way
But it's hard to move on, when the heart is still in disarray

It's all over, and I'm left to mourn the loss
Of a love that we had, and the love that we couldn't cross
But even in the sorrow, there's a glimmer of hope
A chance to start anew, and find a way to cope

So I'll take a deep breath, and let the tears fall like rain
And I'll whisper a final goodbye, to the love that we couldn't sustain
It's all over, and it's time to move on
But in my heart, the memories of our love will forever be strong.

Pain

A sharp stab in the heart, a piercing scream in the night
A constant reminder, of the hurt that won't take flight
It's a weight that's crushing me, a burden that's hard to bear
A pain that's gnawing at my soul, and leaving me with nothing to share

It's a fire that's burning deep, a flame that's burning bright
A passion that's turned to ash, a love that's lost its light
It's a wound that won't heal, a scar that won't fade
A pain that's etched on my heart, and forever will be displayed

I try to hide it, to mask it with a smile
But it's hard to conceal, the hurt that's lingering for a while
It's a ache that's always there, a throb that won't subside
A pain that's my constant companion, my shadow that won't divide

It's a reminder of what's lost, of what could never be
A bittersweet memory, of what used to be
It's a longing that's unfulfilled, a yearning that's unmet
A pain that's my reality, my heart's regret

But even in the pain, there's a beauty to be found
A strength that's born of suffering, a heart that's turned around
It's a chance to learn and grow, to rise above the pain
To find a way to heal, to love again, to live again

So I'll hold on to the pain, and let it shape me anew
I'll use it to fuel my journey, to find my way to you
I'll turn the hurt into hope, the sorrow into song
And I'll rise above the pain, and find where I belong

For pain is a part of life, a thread in the tapestry
A reminder of our humanity, a symbol of our fragility
But it's also a chance to grow, to learn and to explore
To find the strength in our weakness, and to rise above the pain once
more.

Never Too Late

In the quiet hush of evening's veil,
When shadows linger, hearts mayall,
A whisper rides the soft night air,
"Awake, dear soul, life's treasures are rare."

The dreams deferred, like leaves in fall,
Wait patiently, they siren-call,
Each sigh of time, each passing day,
Is but a canvas where hopes may play.

With every wrinkle, wisdom's thread,
Weaving stories of what lies ahead,
Each heartbeat counts in rhythms sweet,
Reminds us, dear, it's never too late.

There's beauty in the scars we bear,
In roads less traveled, in love laid bare,
When daylight wanes and doubts invade,
Trust the glow within that won't soon fade.

For seasons change with grace's hand,
What once seemed lost can bloom and stand,
The heart, a compass, knows its way,
Through stormy nights to bright-lit days.

So rise, dear dreamer; don't hesitate,
The clock may tick, but never berate,
For every dawn, a fresh embrace,
In the tapestry of time, you find your place.

Fear not the years that passed you by,
For sunsets cradle the open sky,
And as the stars ignite the slate,
Remember always: it's never too late.

On My Own

In the quiet cradle of the night,
Where whispers weave with dreams not yet born,
I step into the shadows of my soul,
Untangling the threads of the world, worn.

A tapestry of thoughts, a colorful plight,
Each hue a story, every thread forlorn,
The laughter that danced in the light of the day,
Now sighs in the silence, a heart gently torn.

I walk through the echoes of what used to be,
Through valleys of sorrow, up mountains of hope.
Each step on this path, a testament true,
In solitude's grip, I learn how to cope.

Here, in the stillness, I find a soft voice,
It whispers of strength, of courage, of grace.
In the depths of my heart, I am not alone,
For within me, the shadows hold light's embrace.

With ink on my fingers, I carve out the pain,
Each word a release, a feathered escape.
The poems that rise like smoke in the air,
Are fragments of me, my essence, my shape.

No longer a wanderer, lost in the crowd,
I'll honor my journey, embrace the unknown.
For in every heart, there's a story unsung,
A rhythm, a pulse, a love to be grown.

So here with my pen, under stars that ignite,
I dance with my fears, with passions unchained.
On my own, yet together, with every soul's song,
In the tapestry of life, our hearts will remain.

In The Heart Of The Riot

In the city's pulse, where shadows convulse,
Beneath a sky bruised with ash and despair,
Voices rise deafening, a cacophony,
Each heartbeats' cry, ignited to dare.

Steel and whispers, they clash in the night,
A million hopes straining against iron bars,
Fists like thunder, emotions ablaze,
Rebellion's child beneath blood-stained stars.

Echoes of justice linger like smoke,
As laughter blurs with the sorrowful wails,
A dance of the restless, the brave, the unheard,
United in fury, defiance prevails.

Hands reach for freedom, for light in the gloom,
While memories linger of silence, of shame,
The air thick with anguish, yet fervor sparks bright,
For change wears the mask of a weary refrain.

Yet, among the chaos, a glimmer emerges,
A symphony swelling with dreams of the brave,
In the heart of the riot, a promise ignites,
For every lost soul, a future to save.

In every burnt corner, new seeds take their flight,
At dawn, we'll emerge, unfurling our wings,
What once was a riot, now echoes of change,
In the heart of the storm, a new anthem sings.

Get Out Alive

In the depths of darkness, I wander and roam
A world of shadows, where danger is home
Every step forward, a risk I must take
To escape the silence, for my soul's sake

The city's cold whisper, a siren's call
Lures me to the edge, where I might take a fall
But I won't back down, I'll face the test
For I must get out alive, and find my best

Through the concrete jungle, I navigate the night
Where dreams and nightmares, in darkness take flight
I push through the struggle, with every breath I make
To rise above the chaos, for my heart's sake

Get out alive, that's my goal
To overcome the obstacles, and reach my soul
To find the light in darkness, the calm in every storm
To rise up, and get out alive, and transform.

Let It Die

Let it die, the flame that flickers bright
A burning ember, lost in endless night
It once warmed hearts and lit the way
But now it casts a fading, dying ray

Let it die, the dream that's lost its charm
A fleeting vision, dispelled by alarm
It once inspired hope and fueled the soul
But now it's just a memory, growing old

Let it die, the love that's lost its fire
A smoldering ash, that once aspired
To burn with passion, and never subside
But now it's just a whisper, a dying tide

Let it die, and from its ashes cold
A new spark may ignite, a new story unfold
For in the darkness, there's a chance to begin
To let go of the past, and start anew within.

Over And Over

In circles we wander, lost and alone
Trapped in the cycle, of our own making known
We search for a way out, a path to break free
But like a maze, it leads us back to where we used to be

Over and over, we relive the same
Mistakes and heartaches, like a never-ending game
We try to learn from them, to grow and to mend
But like a shadow, they follow us, until the end

In the mirror's reflection, a familiar face stares
A prisoner of habits, and the weight of our cares
We yearn to break the chains, to shatter the mold
But like a song on repeat, our story's told

Over and over, the wheel spins round
A never-ending cycle, of love and loss, and sound
Yet in the repetition, a rhythm can be found
A beat that echoes hope, a melody that turns us around.

Time Of Dying

In twilight's hush, where shadows play
A whispered warning, of life's fleeting day
The wind it howls, like a mournful sigh
As petals drop, and leaves say goodbye

The time of dying, a season's sway
A final farewell, to life's vibrant ray
The sun sets low, in a fiery blaze
As darkness gathers, in a dying daze

Memories linger, like autumn's decay
Fading light, on a life's final day
The heart beats slow, in a mournful pace
As the soul prepares, for its final place

In this time of dying, we search for peace
A calm within, the turmoil's wild release
A chance to let go, of life's troubled sea
And find solace, in eternity.

Gone Forever

In the silence, I hear your name
A whispered echo, a lingering flame
But like the wind, you're gone, lost in the air
Leaving me with nothing, but a hollow stare

Memories of you, they still remain
A bittersweet reminder, of joy and pain
But like the seasons, you've faded away
And I'm left to wonder, if you'll ever stay

In dreams, I see your face, a fleeting glance
A moment's beauty, a lifetime's dance
But when I wake, you're gone, lost in the night
And I'm left to sorrow, without a fight

Gone forever, like the morning dew
Lost in the shadows, where love once shone true
In my heart, a piece of you will stay
But like the stars, you're gone, faded away.

Running Away

I'm chasing shadows, I'm fleeing the light
I'm running away, from the darkness of night
I'm searching for solace, for a place to hide
From the ghosts that haunt me, from the demons inside

My feet pound the pavement, my heart beats like a drum
I'm running from the memories, from the love that's gone
I'm trying to escape, from the pain and the shame
But like a mirror's reflection, it's always the same

I'm running through the city, through the streets and the pain
I'm trying to find my way, through the darkness and the rain
I'm searching for a refuge, for a place to call home
But like a will-o'-the-wisp, it's always just out of reach, unknown

I'll keep on running, through the night and the day
I'll keep on searching, for a way to escape
But like a maze with no exit, I'll always find my way
Back to the starting point, where the darkness holds sway.

Bitter Taste

On my lips, a bitter taste
A flavor of sorrow, a hint of waste
A reminder of love that's lost its way
A memory of joy that's faded away

Like a cup of coffee, left to grow cold
Our love has stagnated, its flavors grown old
The sweetness has turned, to a bitter regret
A longing for what's lost, a yearning to forget

In the shadows, I search for the light
A guiding star, to lead me through the night
But like a mirage, it vanishes from sight
Leaving me with nothing, but the bitter taste of flight

Time may heal the wounds, but it won't erase
The bitter taste of love, that's been replaced
By the emptiness of loss, the hollow of despair
A flavor that lingers, a reminder of what's not there.

Break

A crack in the mirror, a shatter of glass
A reflection of shards, a broken past
The pieces fall slowly, like tears from above
A fragile heart breaking, a soul losing its love

The weight of the world, crushes down on me
A burden too heavy, a load I can't see
The chains that bind me, the ropes that hold tight
A suffocating grip, that's squeezing out the light

I need a break, a chance to breathe
A moment to escape, from this endless siege
A respite from the pain, a reprieve from the strife
A break from the heartache, a chance to rediscover life

So I'll take a step back, and let the pieces fall
I'll shatter the illusions, and let the truth stand tall
I'll break free from the shackles, and spread my wings to fly
And maybe, just maybe, I'll find my way to the other side.

World So Cold

Frosty winds they whisper, through the city's endless grey
A chill that cuts to the bone, a world that's gone astray
The hearts of strangers passing, like shadows on the wall
No warmth, no love, no kindness, in this world so cold after all

The fire that once burned bright, has flickered out to sea
Leaving only embers, of a love that used to be
The smiles that once lit up, the darkest of nights
Now frozen in a glare, of icy, loveless lights

In this world so cold, we're lost and alone
Adrift in a sea of faces, that are made of stone
We search for a haven, a place to call our own
But like a winter's dawn, it's hard to find a place to call home

Yet still we hold on to hope, a flame that flickers bright
A beacon in the darkness, that guides us through the night
And though the world may seem, so cold and unforgiving too
There's still a love that's burning, a heart that's still true.

Lost In You

In the depths of your eyes, I drown
A sea of emotions, where I'm lost and found
The waves of your touch, they crash on the shore
And I'm swept away, to a place I've never known before

Your lips, a whispered promise, of a love so true
A gentle breeze that soothes, and calms my soul anew
Your skin, a canvas of beauty, where art and love entwine
And I'm lost in the masterpiece, of your heart and mine

In the silence of the night, I hear your voice so clear
A whispered lullaby, that calms my deepest fear
Your love, a guiding star, that shines so bright and bold
And I'm lost in the navigation, of our hearts, forever to unfold

In your arms, I find my home, a place where I am free
A sanctuary of love, where I can be me
Lost in you, I find myself, in the depths of your eyes
And in your love, I am forever lost in the surprise.

The Good Life

A warm sun on my skin, a gentle breeze in my hair
A sense of peace that settles, without a single care
A cup of coffee in my hand, a good book by my side
A feeling of contentment, that I've never known to divide

A loving partner to share, in the joys and the strife
A family that's always there, to support and to thrive in life
Friends who laugh and love and live, with hearts that are true and kind
A community that welcomes, with open arms and open mind

A home that's warm and cozy, with a fireplace that crackles bright
A garden that blooms with beauty, in the morning's golden light
A life that's filled with purpose, with passions that ignite
A sense of fulfillment that comes, from living life with all my might

This is the good life, the one that I adore
A life that's simple, yet rich, and forever in store
A life that's filled with love and laughter, with adventure and with glee
The good life, the one that's mine, and the one that's meant to be.

No More

No more tears to cry, no more pain to bear
No more heartache, no more sorrow to share
The weight of the world, it no longer presses down
The chains that bound me, they're broken, and I'm free to drown

No more lies to tell, no more secrets to keep
No more pretending, no more masks to reap
The truth it sets me free, it's a burden I no longer bear
I'm unshackled from the past, and I'm no longer trapped there

No more sleepless nights, no more endless fights
No more walking on eggshells, no more living in fright
The calm it soothes my soul, it's a peace that I've never known
I'm finally home, and I'm no longer alone

No more, the words echo, like a mantra in my mind
A reminder of the freedom, that I've left behind
The ghosts of my past, they no longer haunt me still
I'm finally free, and I'm living life at will.

Last To Know

I was the last to know, the last to see
The truth that was hiding, behind you and me
I was the last to hear, the whispers and the lies
The secrets that were kept, behind closed eyes

I was the last to feel, the weight of the pain
The heartache that was coming, like a summer rain
I was the last to realize, the love that was lost
The memories that were fading, like the morning frost

I was the last to know, the truth that you concealed
The love that you pretended, the heart that you revealed
I was the last to see, the emptiness in your eyes
The love that had died, and the goodbye that you denied

But now I know the truth, and I'm finally free
From the chains that bound me, from the love that was a lie to me
I'm the last to know, but I'm the first to see
That I deserve better, and that's just me.

Someone Who Cares

In a world that's full of strangers, I search for a friendly face
A gentle soul who'll listen, and take the time to know my place
Someone who'll hear my whispers, and feel my deepest pain
And offer a comforting presence, that will soothe my heart and soul again

Someone who'll stand by my side, through life's joys and its fears
Who'll hold my hand when I'm trembling, and wipe away my tears
Someone who'll celebrate with me, in times of triumph and delight
And offer a shoulder to lean on, when the darkness of night takes flight

In a world that's full of noise, I yearn for a quiet friend
Someone who'll sit with me in silence, until the stormy weather ends
Someone who'll see beyond my surface, and touch the depths of my heart
And love me for who I am, and never depart

If you're someone who cares, then I need you by my side
To walk with me through life's journey, and be my guiding light
I need someone who'll care for me, and show me love that's true
And if that someone is you, then I'll be forever grateful to you.

Bully

Words cut deep, like a knife in the dark
A whispered taunt, a jeer, a cruel spark
A heart that's heavy, with the weight of the pain
A soul that's weary, from the constant strain

You think you're strong, with your words so bold
But your heart is weak, with a spirit that's cold
You prey on the vulnerable, with a cruel delight
But your own fears and doubts, are the demons you fight

You may have power, but it's a fleeting thing
For the words you speak, will one day be your sting
You may have control, but it's a fragile hold
For the hearts you break, will one day be your gold

But to the ones you've hurt, I want you to know
That you may have broken, but you'll never own
Their hearts, their souls, their spirits so bright
For they will rise above, and shine with all their might

And to the bully, I say, it's time to cease
Your words, your actions, your cruel release
For the power is not yours, but theirs to claim
And they will rise up, and their voices will proclaim.

Without You

My world is empty, my heart is bare
The silence is deafening, without you there
The shadows that dance, upon the wall
Remind me of your laughter, and the love that we once called

The city streets are crowded, but I feel alone
The noise of the traffic, is a hollow, echoing tone
I search for your smile, in the faces that I see
But it's just a fleeting glimpse, of what used to be

My days are filled with longing, my nights with tears
I'm left to wonder, why you disappeared
The memories of our love, they linger on my mind
A bittersweet reminder, of what we left behind

Without you, life is dull, the colors are gray
The music that we danced to, is now just a faded way
I'm left to pick up the pieces, of a love that's lost its way
And find a new tomorrow, without you, day by day.

Going Down

I'm falling, falling, down the darkest night
A spiral staircase, with no end in sight
The walls are closing in, the air is thick with pain
I'm searching for a lifeline, but it's slipping through my brain

The city lights are blurring, like a watercolor stain
The sounds of the world, are a distant, fading strain
I'm losing my grip, on the things that I hold dear
I'm slipping under, into the darkness, and the fear

I try to cry out, but my voice is lost in the haze
I try to reach out, but my hands are grasping at the daze
I'm going down, down, into the abyss
A never-ending descent, into the darkness, and the mess

But still I hold on, to the hope that I'll be free
That someday I'll rise up, and shine like I used to be
That someday I'll find my way, out of this darkest night
And I'll emerge into the light, and shine with all my might.

Life Starts Now

The clock strikes zero, a new beginning unfolds
A chapter closed, a new story to be told
The past is behind me, with all its joy and pain
But life starts now, and I'm ready to begin again

The sun rises slowly, over the morning dew
A fresh canvas awaits, with colors anew
The world awakens, with a vibrant, pulsing beat
And I step forward, with a heart that skips a treat

The possibilities stretch, like a horizon so wide
A blank page waiting, for the story I'll provide
The choices I make, will shape the road ahead
And I'm ready to take, the first step into the unknown instead

Life starts now, with every breath I take
A new chance to rediscover, the beauty I'll make
To learn, to grow, to love, to live and to thrive
To make this life, the one I've always wanted to arrive

So here I stand, at the threshold of this new day
Ready to embark, on this journey, in a brand new way
Life starts now, and I'm ready to begin
To write the story of this life I'm living within.

The High Road

I choose to take the high road, where the air is crisp and clean
Where the view is breathtaking, and my heart can be serene
I leave the noise behind, the chaos and the pain
And find my peace of mind, on this winding road I've gained

I won't engage in the drama, or stoop to the lowest blow
I'll rise above the negativity, and let my spirit glow
I'll take the path that's less traveled, where the journey isn't so worn
And find my own way, to a place where love is born

The high road is not always easy, it's steep and winding too
But the view from the top, is a sight that's forever true
It's a place where I can breathe, where my heart can be free
And I can find my inner peace, wild and carefree

I'll take the high road, and I'll walk it with pride
With my head held high, and my heart full of love inside
I'll leave the hate behind, and I'll rise above the pain
And I'll find my way, to a place where love will reign.

Give In To Me

Give in to me, let go of your fears
Let the walls come down, and dry away your tears
I'll take your hand, and lead you through the night
And guide you to a place, where love shines with all its light

Give in to me, and let our hearts collide
Let the passion ignite, and our love abide
I'll hold you close, and whisper in your ear
And tell you all the secrets, that only lovers share

Give in to me, and let our love be free
Let's dance beneath the stars, and wild and carelessly
I'll take your breath away, with every kiss and every touch
And give you all the love, that you've been searching for so much

Give in to me, and let our love shine bright
Let's chase the sunrise, and make this night last all life
I'll love you till the end, of time and space and sea
And give you all the love, that's meant to be.

Happiness

Happiness is a whisper, a gentle summer breeze
That rustles through the leaves, and brings a sense of ease
It's a warm and fuzzy feeling, that spreads from head to toe
A sense of joy and contentment, that makes the heart glow

Happiness is a smile, that creeps upon the face
A laugh that echoes loudly, and a sense of time and space
It's a feeling that's contagious, that spreads like wildfire's flame
A sense of joy and wonder, that's felt by all who know its name

Happiness is a choice, that we make every single day
A decision to see the beauty, in every single way
It's a mindset and a attitude, that we cultivate with care
A sense of joy and gratitude, that's always present and aware

Happiness is a journey, that we embark upon with glee
A path that winds and turns, through hills and valleys we'll see
It's a adventure that's full of surprises, full of twists and turns
A sense of joy and wonder, that forever yearns and burns

So let's choose happiness, every single day
Let's spread joy and love, in every single way
Let's cultivate a mindset, that's full of gratitude and cheer
And let's embark upon the journey of happiness that's always near.

Give Me A Reason

Give me a reason to stay, to fight another day
To hold on to hope, when the darkness fades away
Give me a reason to believe, that things will get better still
To trust that the heartache, will eventually heal and fulfill

Give me a reason to love, to open up my heart
To let someone in, and never be apart
Give me a reason to dream, to chase the impossible high
To reach for the stars, and never say goodbye

Give me a reason to live, to find my purpose and my place
To make a difference, and leave a lasting trace
Give me a reason to smile, to laugh and to be free
To find my happiness, and live wild and carelessly

Give me a reason, just one, to keep on moving forward still
To face the unknown, and conquer the hills
Give me a reason, and I'll hold on tight
And I'll keep on fighting, for the light.

Time That Remains

The clock ticks on, the hours slip away
The time that remains, is fleeting, day by day
I cherish every moment, every second I share
For the time that remains, is a gift beyond compare

Memories linger, of laughter and of tears
Of moments I've lived, through all the passing years
I hold them close, and treasure them with care
For the time that remains, is a time to show I truly care

The future beckons, with possibilities untold
A chapter yet unwritten, with stories yet untold
I'll make the most of the time, that remains to me
And fill each moment, with love, laughter, and glee

The time that remains, is a gift so rare
A chance to live, to love, to laugh, and to share
I'll use each moment wisely, and make it truly mine
And cherish the time that remains, until the end of time.

Expectations

Expectations, like shadows on the wall
Looming large, and threatening to enthrall
The weight of what's anticipated, the pressure to conform
A burden to bear, that can be hard to transform

We're shaped by what's expected, by the norms and the rules
By the standards we're held to, and the judgments that cool
Our passions and desires, our dreams and our fire
Can be dimmed by the expectations, that we're forced to acquire

But what of our own desires, our own hearts' deepest cry?
Do we dare to defy the expectations that pass us by?
Or do we conform, and fit into the mold?
And sacrifice our own truth, to a story that's been told?

Expectations, like chains that bind and restrict
Can stifle our growth, and our souls' deepest instinct
To break free from the mold, to shatter the glass ceiling high
And rise up to our true selves, with a voice that won't deny.

Broken Glass

Shards of glass, like tears that fall
Scattered on the floor, beyond recall
A reflection of the heart, that's lost its way
A fragment of a dream, that's shattered, day by day

Memories linger, like the scent of smoke
A reminder of what's been, and what's been spoke
The whispers of the past, that echo through the mind
A bittersweet reminder, of love and loss entwined

Like broken glass, our hearts can shatter and break
Leaving scars that never heal, and a pain that won't abate
But even in the shards, there's a beauty to behold
A reflection of the love, that once made us whole

So let's gather up the pieces, and try to make amends
For in the broken glass, we'll find the love that never ends
And though it may be shattered, it's still a work of art
A testament to love, that's forever in our heart.

Unbreakable Heart

My heart is made of steel, forged in the fire of pain
Unbreakable and strong, it beats with a love that remains
Through every stormy night, through every darkest day
It holds on to hope, and never fades away

It's been battered and bruised, it's been broken and worn
But still it beats with courage, and a love that's born
Of every tear I've cried, of every sorrow I've known
My heart has been made stronger, and it's love has been made grown

I've been through the fire, and I've been through the rain
But my heart remains unbroken, and it's love remains the same
It's a flame that burns so brightly, a beacon in the night
Guiding me through the darkness, and shining with all its might

My heart is unbreakable, it's a fortress strong and true
A sanctuary of love, where dreams and hope shine through
It's a heart that's made of steel, but it's also made of gold
A treasure trove of love that will never grow old.

Fallen Angel

In twilight's hush, where shadows play
A figure falls, from a heavenly way
Once a being of light, with wings so bright
Now a soul cast down, in the dark of night

With eyes that once shone, like stars in the sky
Now dimmed with sorrow, and a tear-stained sigh
The fallen angel, with a heart so sore
Laments the loss, of a love that's no more

In heaven's realm, a seat was reserved
But now it's empty, and the angel's deserved
A fate that's cruel, a punishment so cold
For a love that was forbidden, and a heart that's grown old

The fallen angel, with a spirit so bold
Now walks the earth, with a story untold
A tale of love and loss, of heaven and hell
A testament to the heart, that beats within the shell

But still the angel holds, on to love's pure light
A beacon in the darkness, that guides through the night
And though the wings may be, broken and worn
The heart remains unbroken, and the love remains reborn.

Tell Me Why

Tell me why the stars shine bright in the midnight sky
Tell me why the ocean waves crash, and then gently sigh
Tell me why the wind whispers secrets, as it blows through the trees
Tell me why the heart beats with a love, that brings us to our knees

Tell me why we search for answers, in the darkness and the light
Tell me why we yearn for connection, through the endless night
Tell me why we chase the dreams, that we've yet to define
Tell me why we hold on to hope, when the world is on our mind

Tell me why the sun rises, over the mountains high
Tell me why the rain falls gently, and brings new life to the sky
Tell me why the heart breaks, with a sorrow so true
Tell me why we find our way, through the darkness, to a love that shines
through

Tell me why, oh tell me why, the mysteries of life unfold
Tell me why, oh tell me why, our hearts beat with a love so bold
Perhaps the answer lies, in the questions that we ask
Perhaps the truth is found, in the love that we hold, and the hearts that
we task.

One Too Many

One too many tears have fallen, like the autumn rain
One too many heartaches, that refuse to wane
One too many lies have been told, in the dead of night
One too many promises broken, without a fight

One too many doors have been closed, with a slam and a sigh
One too many windows shattered, with a heartbreaking cry
One too many dreams have been lost, like grains of sand
One too many hopes have been crushed, by a heavy hand

One too many times I've been left, to pick up the pieces of me
One too many times I've been hurt, and left to wonder why it's me
One too many times I've been fooled, by a love that wasn't true
One too many times I've been broken, and left to break through

But still I rise, like the morning sun
Still I heal, like the wounds that are slowly undone
Still I love, like the heart that beats within
Still I hope, like the dreams that I hold, and the love that I win.

The End Is Not The Answer

The end is not the answer, to the questions that we seek
For in the final moment, we find only what we speak
The end is not the destination, but a journey to unfold
A chapter in the story, of a life that's yet untold

The end is not the closure, that we think it will bring
For in the silence that follows, our hearts keep on singing
The end is not the goodbye, that we fear it will be
But a hello to a new dawn, and a chance to be free

The end is not the answer, to the mysteries of life
For in the unknown that lies, beyond the final strife
We find the truth that we seek, in the love that we hold dear
And the memories that we cherish, and the laughter that we hear

So let us not be fooled, by the end that we see
For in the darkness that it brings, there's a light that's yet to be
And though it may seem final, it's just a new beginning's birth
The end is not the answer, but a doorway to the earth.

I'm An Outsider

I'm an outsider, looking in
A stranger in a world that spins
I don't fit the mold, I don't conform
I'm a rebel heart, beating to a different form

I see the world, through different eyes
A perspective unique, a soul that compromises
I walk the fine line, between the light and the dark
A balancing act, between the heart and the spark

I'm an outsider, with a voice unheard
A whisper in the wind, a cry that's blurred
I'm a dreamer, a thinker, a soul on fire
A heart that beats with passion, a spirit that aspires

I'm an outsider, but I'm not alone
There are others like me, who roam
We're the misfits, the outcasts, the ones who don't belong
But we're the ones who see, the world from a different song

So I'll keep on walking, this path that's mine
A journey of self-discovery, a soul that's divine
I'll keep on being, an outsider, proud and free
A heart that beats with individuality.

Nothing To Lose But You

In the depths of my soul, there's a fire that burns
A flame that flickers bright, with a passion that yearns
To break free from the chains, that bind me to the ground
To rise up and take flight, with a heart that's unbound

I've got nothing to lose, but the weight that I carry
The burden of my doubts, the fears that make me wary
I've got nothing to lose, but the ghosts that haunt my past
The shadows that creep in, and the love that didn't last

But I've got everything to gain, by letting go of the pain
By embracing the unknown, and the love that remains
I've got everything to gain, by taking a chance on you
By risking it all, and seeing this love shine through

So I'll take the leap of faith, and jump into the night
With a heart that's full of hope, and a soul that's alight
I'll take the risk, and roll the dice, with a love that's true
And I'll gamble everything, on the chance that I'll spend forever with
you.

Me Against You

Me against you, a battle to be won
A war of words, a clash of wills, before the day is done
I stand my ground, with feet firmly planted wide
While you oppose me, with a determination to divide

The lines are drawn, the stakes are high
The tension builds, as our hearts beat by
I see the fire, in your eyes so bright
But I won't back down, without a fight

Me against you, a test of strength and might
A challenge to our hearts, to see who'll hold on tight
I'll stand my ground, and fight for what I believe
While you'll push back hard, with a passion that you can't leave

But in the heat, of this battle we wage
I see a glimmer, of a love that's hard to engage
A love that's hidden, beneath the surface so bright
A love that's waiting, to be ignited in the night

So let's lay down, our arms and our pride
And find a love, that will be our guide
For me against you, is just a game we play
But love between us can show us a brighter way.

Love Me Or Leave Me

Love me or leave me, the choice is yours to make
But don't pretend to love me, with a heart that's about to break
I need your love to be real, to be true and pure of heart
Not a love that's conditional, or one that will depart

I'll take the risk of being hurt, of being left behind
But I won't settle for a love, that's not truly mine
I'll take the chance of loving you, with every fiber of my soul
But you must meet me halfway, with a love that makes me whole

Love me or leave me, don't play games with my heart
I'm not a toy to be used, or a love that's torn apart
I'm a woman who deserves, to be loved with every breath
To be cherished, honored, and loved, until my dying death

So love me or leave me, the choice is yours to make
But know that I'll not settle, for a love that's fake
I'll hold out for the real thing, for a love that's true and kind
And if that's not what you offer, then I'll leave you behind.

Strange Days

Strange days, we're living in strange days
Where the world outside is spinning in crazy ways
The rules don't apply, the norms are all awry
We're navigating uncharted waters, with a lonely sigh

The skies are gray, the sun is hiding its face
The winds are howling, with a mournful, eerie pace
The earth is shaking, with a rumble and a roar
We're living in strange days, where nothing seems sure anymore

The news is filled, with stories of strife and pain
The world is divided, with a chasm that's hard to explain
We're searching for answers, but they're hard to find
We're living in strange days, where the truth is left behind

But even in the chaos, there's a beauty to be found
A resilience of spirit, that's turning the world around
A chance to redefine, what's truly important to us all
A time to come together, and stand tall

So let's navigate, these strange and uncertain days
With hearts that are open, and minds that are raised
Let's find the love and kindness, that's hidden deep inside

And let's make our way, through these strange days, with a heart full of pride.

Neurotic

My mind is a maze, a labyrinth of fear
A never-ending cycle, of anxiety and tears
I'm trapped in my thoughts, a prisoner of my own
A neurotic nightmare, that I've never known

I overthink and overanalyze, every single thing
I read between the lines, and hear what's left unsaid
I'm a master of catastrophizing, a virtuoso of doom
I'm a neurotic mess, in a world that's moving too soon

My heart is a battleground, where emotions clash and fight
A war zone of worries, where the enemy is always in sight
I'm a soldier in the trenches, fighting for my sanity
A neurotic warrior, armed with nothing but my anxiety

But still I hold on tight, to the hope that I'll be free
From this neurotic hell, that's been haunting me
I'll find my way out, of this maze of fear and doubt
And I'll learn to quiet, the voices that scream and shout

So I'll take a deep breath, and let the calm wash over me
And I'll remind myself, that I'm strong and I'm free
I'll rise above the noise, and shine like the sun in the sea
And I'll leave my neurosis, where it belongs – in history.

Lifetime

A lifetime of memories, etched on my soul
Moments of joy and laughter, forever to unfold
A lifetime of love and loss, of triumph and defeat
A story of trials and tribulations, that I've lived to repeat

A lifetime of dreams and desires, that I've yet to fulfill
A bucket list of adventures, that I hope to still
A lifetime of regrets and what-ifs, that I've learned to release
A journey of self-discovery, that's brought me to my knees

A lifetime of relationships, that have shaped me into who I am
A tapestry of friendships, that have been woven like a clan
A lifetime of family ties, that bind me to my past
A heritage of love and legacy, that will forever last

A lifetime of moments, that I'll always treasure and hold
A collection of snapshots, that tell the story of my soul
A lifetime of experiences, that have made me who I am today
A journey of growth and learning, that will continue on my way

So let me cherish every moment, and hold them dear to my heart
For a lifetime of memories, it is a treasure to never depart.

A Scar Is Born

A scar is born, from the wounds of the past
A reminder of the pain, that will forever last
A mark on the skin, a memory in the mind
A testament to the hurt, that we've left behind

It starts as a cut, a gash, a tear
A moment of vulnerability, a lifetime to repair
The skin begins to heal, but the scar remains
A constant reminder, of the pain that we've sustained

But scars are not just physical, they can be emotional too
A heart that's been broken, a spirit that's been bruised and blue
The memories of the hurt, they linger and they stay
A scar that's born, from the wounds of yesterday

Yet even in the scarring, there's a beauty to behold
A story of survival, of strength and of gold
For every scar that's born, is a testament to our might
A reminder that we've lived, and that we've made it through the night

So let us wear our scars, with pride and with honor true
For they are a part of us, and a story that's still being written anew.

No Tomorrow

There's no tomorrow, only today
A fleeting moment, that slips away
No promises of dawn, no guarantees of night
Just the present moment, shining with all its light

I'll take the time I have, and make the most of it
I'll cherish every second, and never quit
I'll live for now, and not for what's to come
For in the end, it's not the years that we live, but the life that we've
become

There's no tomorrow, to put things off until
No next time, no second chance, no final will
So I'll take the leap, and make the jump
I'll seize the day, and make my own luck

I'll love with all my heart, and give with all my soul
I'll live each day as if it's my last, and make it whole
I'll take the risk, and face the fear
For in the end, it's not the years that we live, but the life that we hold
dear

So let's make the most, of this one precious day
Let's live it to the fullest, in every single way

For there's no tomorrow, to fall back on
Only today, and the life that we've just begun.

Redemption

In the depths of darkness, where shadows roam
I found myself lost, with no way to call home
The weight of my mistakes, crushed me to the ground
And I thought all was lost, with no redemption to be found

But then I saw a glimmer, of hope in the night
A chance to make amends, and shine with new light
I took the first step forward, on a journey to redeem
And with each step I took, I felt my heart start to beam

The chains that bound me, began to break apart
As I faced my demons, and found the courage to start
A new path unfolded, with a chance to begin anew
And I walked with a purpose, with redemption shining through

With every step I took, I felt my soul revive
As I left the darkness behind, and stepped into the light alive
I found forgiveness, and a chance to make things right
And I knew that I was worthy, of a second chance to take flight

Redemption's sweet solace, wrapped around my heart
A reminder that I'm worthy, of a brand new start
I'll hold on to this hope, and never let it fade
For redemption's promise, has given me a new way.

Chain of Abuse

A chain of abuse, forged in pain and fear
Link by link, it binds us, year after year
A cycle of hurt, that's hard to break
A legacy of suffering, that's passed down, for our sake

It starts with a whisper, a subtle, cruel tone
A belittling remark, that cuts to the bone
A slap, a push, a shove, a blow that knocks us down
A chain of abuse, that wears a wicked crown

It's a chain that's strengthened, by the silence we keep
By the secrets we hide, and the lies we repeat
It's a chain that's forged, in the fire of our shame
A chain that bound us, to the abuse we can't reclaim

But there's a way to break it, to shatter the links that bind
To speak out against the abuse, and leave the shame behind
To seek help and support, to find a voice that's clear
To break the chain of abuse, and wipe away our tears

So let's raise our voices, and shatter the silence and fear
Let's break the chain of abuse, and bring hope and healing near
Let's stand together, and support each other's might
Let's break the chain of abuse, and shine a light on what's right.

Someone To Talk To

In the silence, I hear my thoughts
A cacophony of emotions, that never stop
I search for a voice, a listening ear
Someone to talk to, who'll calm my fear

The weight of the world, it presses down
A burden I carry, with no one around
To share the load, to ease the pain
Someone to talk to, who'll help me regain

In the stillness of night, I feel alone
The city sleeps, but my heart is a stone
I yearn for connection, for a human touch
Someone to talk to, who'll hear me so much

Then I find a friend, a listening soul
Someone who cares, who makes me whole
They hear my words, my fears, my tears
And with their kindness, calm my doubts and fears

With someone to talk to, the world's a lighter load
The burden shared, the pain's eased, I'm no longer alone
I find my voice, my strength, my heart
With someone to talk to, we'll never be apart.

Emotions

Emotions, a rollercoaster ride
Twisting and turning, with no place to hide
They come and they go, like the ebb and the flow
Leaving me breathless, with a heart that's aglow

Joy, a spark of sunshine, that brightens up my day
A smile that creeps, and a laugh that finds its way
But then sorrow creeps in, like a thief in the night
Stealing my happiness, and leaving me with a fight

Fear, a whisper in my ear, that makes my heart skip a beat
A doubt that creeps in, and makes my soul retreat
But then courage finds its voice, and stands up tall and strong
And I face my fears, and sing a brand new song

Love, a flame that burns, a fire that never fades
A warmth that spreads, and a heart that's not afraid
To give and to receive, to open up and be
A love that's pure and true, and sets my soul free

Emotions, a journey through, the ups and the downs
A ride that's unpredictable, but always wears a crown
For in the end, it's not the emotions that define
But how we face them, and make them align.

Is Anybody There?

In the silence, I call out loud
Is anybody there? Can anybody hear my crowd?
I'm searching for a voice, a friendly face
A connection to the world, a sense of time and space

I'm lost in the darkness, with no guiding light
I'm reaching out for someone, to hold on tight
I'm yearning for a whisper, a gentle, soothing tone
To let me know I'm not alone

Is anybody there? Can anybody see?
The emptiness I'm feeling, the loneliness that's me?
I'm trying to find my way, through the noise and the pain
But it's hard to keep going, when I feel so alone again

Then I hear a whisper, a soft and gentle sound
A voice that's whispering, "You're not alone, you're found"
A presence that's surrounding me, a love that's shining bright
A sense of peace that's washing over me, like a warm and comforting light

Is anybody there? Yes, somebody's there
A presence that's always with me, a love that's always fair
So I'll hold on to hope, and never give up the fight

For I know that I'm not alone, and that somebody's there to hold me tight.

Heretics And Killers

In the shadows of history, they lurk and they hide
Heretics and killers, with blood on their hands and pride
They've brought forth the darkness, with every cruel deed
Leaving scars that won't heal, and a world in dire need

With torches and pitchforks, they've hunted down the brave
Those who dared to challenge, the status quo they crave
They've silenced the voices, of those who spoke out loud
And brought forth a silence, that's deafening and proud

Their legacy of hatred, lives on through the ages
A stain on humanity, that turns the pages
Of a book that's written, in the blood of the slain
A testament to the darkness, that they've brought forth in vain

But still we rise up, against the forces of night
We stand with the heretics, who dared to shine a light
We honor the martyrs, who gave their lives for the cause
And we'll keep on fighting, for a world that's just and flaws

For in the end it's not, the heretics and killers who'll win
But the brave and the noble, who'll rise up and begin
A new chapter in history, where love and kindness will reign
And the darkness of hatred will be but a distant, fading stain.

Divinity Within

In the depths of my soul, a spark is aglow
A flame that flickers, with a gentle, loving flow
It's the divinity within, a presence so divine
A guiding light that shines, and makes my heart and soul align

It's the whisper in my ear, that tells me I am enough
A voice that echoes, with a love that's strong and tough
It's the wisdom that I seek, the answers to my prayers
A knowing that's within me, that calms my doubts and fears

In the stillness of the night, I feel its gentle might
A power that's beyond me, yet within me, shining bright
It's the divinity within, a sacred, holy space
A place where love resides, and fills my heart with grace

It's the spark that sets me free, from the chains that bind
A fire that burns within me, and lights up my mind
It's the reminder that I'm not alone, that I'm part of something grand
A universe that's connected, and holds me in its loving hand

So I'll listen to its voice, and follow its gentle lead
I'll trust in its wisdom, and let its love and light proceed
For in the divinity within, I know that I am home
Connected to the universe, and never alone.

Bury The Hatchet

In the depths of our souls, a wound still remains
A scar from the past, that refuses to wane
A hatchet once wielded, with anger and with pain
Now lies rusting, a reminder of the hurt and the strain

But today we gather, to lay the past to rest
To bury the hatchet, and let forgiveness be our guest
We'll dig a hole deep, and place the hatchet inside
And cover it with earth, and let the healing begin to reside

We'll take the first step forward, towards a brighter day
And leave the anger and the hurt, to wither away
We'll choose to let go, of the resentment and the pain
And find the courage to forgive, and to love again

The hatchet's rusty blade, will slowly start to fade
As we cultivate compassion, and let love be our shade
We'll nurture the garden, of our hearts and our minds
And let the beauty of forgiveness, forever be intertwined

So let us bury the hatchet, and let the healing begin
Let us choose to forgive, and to let love and peace spin
For in the act of forgiveness, we find our own release
And the hatchet's rusty blade, becomes a distant, fading peace.

Clarity

In the misty dawn of morning, I search for what is clear
A path unwinding, through the fog that brings me fear
I yearn for clarity, a beacon in the night
To guide me through life's journey, and shine a gentle light

The world outside is noisy, with voices loud and bold
Each one competing, for a space to be told
But in the silence, I find my voice, my heart, my soul
A clarity that emerges, like a river flowing whole

Like a drop of dew on a leaf, clarity glistens bright
Reflecting the beauty, of a world in plain sight
It's the whisper in my ear, that tells me what is true
A gentle reminder, of the path I'm meant to pursue

With clarity, the fog lifts, and the path unwinds
I see the world with new eyes, and a heart that's aligned
I walk with purpose, with each step I take
With clarity guiding me, I find my own unique make

In the stillness, I find my voice, my heart, my way
A clarity that shines, like a sunbeam on a brand new day
And with this clarity, I'll walk, I'll run, I'll fly
With a heart full of purpose, and a soul that's alive.

Without Prejudice

In the garden of humanity, where diversity blooms
I'll walk among the flowers, with an open heart and open rooms
I'll let go of assumptions, and lay down my biased crown
And look at each soul, with fresh eyes, and a heart that's renowned

Without prejudice, I'll see the beauty in every face
A unique and precious individual, in a sacred, sacred space
I'll hear their stories, and listen with an open ear
And let their words and wisdom, dispel the doubts and fears that appear

I'll recognize the inherent worth, of every single soul
A spark of the divine, that makes each heart and spirit whole
I'll celebrate the differences, that make us strong and bright
And honor the common humanity, that unites us in the light

Without prejudice, I'll find the courage to be kind
To stand with those who suffer, and to leave the judgments behind
I'll be an ally and a friend, to those who need a hand
And together we'll create, a world where love and acceptance stand

In this garden of humanity, where love and kindness grow
I'll tend the soil with compassion, and watch the beauty unfold and show
Without prejudice, I'll walk, with an open heart and mind
And celebrate the diversity that makes our world so divine.

Mist

The mist descends upon my soul
A gentle veil that makes me whole
It wraps around my heart and mind
A soothing balm that's hard to find

With whispers soft, it calms my fears
And wipes away my doubts and tears
It brings a peace that's hard to know
A stillness that my spirit can't let go

In the mist, I find my way
Through the darkness of each passing day
It guides me through life's troubled sea
And leads me to a place of serenity

The mist reminds me to slow down
To breathe, to pause, to turn around
To see the world with fresh new eyes
And find the beauty that the mist implies

With every step, the mist clears the way
And reveals a path that's new each day
It's a reminder to trust and to believe
That even in uncertainty, I'll find my way to leave

The mist ascends, and slowly fades
Leaving me with a sense of peace that's made
A feeling that remains, long after it's gone
A reminder of the calm that I've known.

Cataract

A veil of misty gray descends
A cataract of cloudy tears that never end
A haze that shrouds the light of day
A dimness that obscures the world's display

Memories of clarity, now distant and past
A faded recollection, that will forever last
The sharpness of vision, lost to the haze
A world that's blurred, in a perpetual daze

But even in the cloudiness, a glimmer shines
A light that breaks through, and redefines
The outlines of reality, and brings them near
A newfound appreciation, for the beauty that's clear

The cataract of time, that clouds our sight
Can't hide the truth, that's waiting to take flight
For even in the dimness, a radiance abides
A light that guides us, through life's ebb and tide

And when the veil is lifted, and the mist clears away
We'll see the world anew, in a brighter, sharper day
The cataract of uncertainty, will be washed clean
And we'll behold the beauty, that's always been.

Harbinger

A whispered warning, on the winds of change
A harbinger of darkness, or a brighter range
A sign of things to come, a messenger of fate
A call to prepare, for the future's uncertain state

With wings of shadow, or feathers of light
The harbinger descends, in the darkness of night
It brings a message, of hope or of despair
A warning to awaken, to the future that's waiting there

A rustling of leaves, a stirring of the trees
A harbinger of autumn, or the summer's gentle breeze
A sign of seasons turning, of cycles yet to come
A reminder to appreciate, the present's fleeting drum

With eyes that see beyond, the veil of time and space
The harbinger gazes, into the future's hidden place
It brings a message, of warning or of cheer
A call to prepare, for the challenges that draw near

So let us heed the harbinger's call
And prepare for the future, with hearts that stand tall
For in its message, we'll find the strength to face
The challenges that lie ahead, in the uncertain, hidden place.

From The Sky

From the sky, a whispered truth
A message carried, on the winds of youth
A gentle breeze that stirs the soul
A reminder of the magic that makes us whole

From the sky, a rainbow's vibrant hue
A symbol of promise, and a beauty shining through
A bridge of colors, that spans the earth and sea
A reminder of the wonders, that await you and me

From the sky, a starry night's twinkling light
A celestial showcase, of the universe's delight
A canopy of diamonds, that sparkles with glee
A reminder of the mysteries, that lie beyond our sea

From the sky, a snowflake's gentle fall
A delicate whisper, of the beauty that stands tall
A fleeting wonder, that melts away with the sun
A reminder of the impermanence, of life's journey just begun

From the sky, a bird's sweet melody
A song of freedom, that echoes wild and carefree
A symphony of joy, that lifts the heart and soul
A reminder of the beauty that makes our spirits whole.

Soliloquy

In the silence of the night, I speak to myself alone
A soliloquy of thoughts, that echo through my soul
A conversation with the shadows, that dance upon the wall
A dialogue of doubts, that whisper through it all

I question my existence, and the purpose that I hold
A search for meaning, in a world that's grown cold
I ponder on the choices, that have led me to this place
A reflection of the moments, that have shaped my face

The darkness listens closely, as I bare my heart and mind
A confessional of sorts, where I leave my fears behind
The silence is a solace, that wraps around my soul
A comforting embrace, that makes me whole

In this soliloquy of mine, I find a strange peace
A sense of clarity, that the world's noise can't release
A understanding of myself, that I've yet to define
A soliloquy that continues, until the morning light is mine

So I'll keep speaking to myself, in the silence of the night
A soliloquy of self-discovery, that shines with all its light
For in the darkness, I find the truth, that sets me free
A soliloquy that's mine alone, a conversation with me.

Reverie

In twilight's hush, where shadows play
I drift away, into a reverie's gray
A world of dreams, where thoughts unfold
A realm of fantasy, where my heart is told

The wind whispers secrets, of far-off lands
And I am transported, to enchanted strands
The stars up above, a twinkling show
A celestial tapestry, that my soul can know

In this reverie, I find my peaceful nest
A haven from the world, where I can rest
My mind wanders freely, through memories and time
And I am one with the universe, in a sweet, sweet rhyme

The world outside recedes, and I am lost in thought
A traveler in the realms, of the imagination's brought
I soar on eagle's wings, through skies of sapphire blue
And my heart is filled, with a sense of wonder anew

In this reverie, I find my creative spark
A flame that flickers brightly, in the dark
It guides me through the night, and leads me to the dawn
And I am reborn, with a heart that's fresh and sworn

So let me drift away, into this reverie's embrace
And let the world outside, fade into a distant space
For in this dreamlike state, I find my heart's delight
And I am one with the universe, in a peaceful, loving light.

Deep Inside

Deep inside, a world is hidden
A realm of emotions, yet unspoken
A labyrinth of thoughts, that twist and turn
A maze of feelings, that yearn to learn

Deep inside, a fire burns so bright
A flame of passion, that guides through the night
A beacon of hope, that shines like a light
A warmth that radiates, and banishes the dark of night

Deep inside, a voice whispers low
A gentle murmur, that only the heart can know
A language of the soul, that speaks directly to the mind
A wisdom that's ancient, and forever left behind

Deep inside, a garden blooms with care
A tapestry of memories, that's woven with love and repair
A sanctuary of peace, that's nurtured through the years
A haven of solace, that calms all doubts and fears

Deep inside, a story waits to be told
A narrative of dreams, that's yet to unfold
A chapter of the heart, that's still being written every day
A tale of love and courage, that's finding its way

So let us venture deep inside
And explore the mysteries, that our hearts abide
For in the depths of our own soul
Lies a world of wonder, that makes us whole.

Consequence

In the wake of our choices, a path is laid
A consequence of actions, that our hearts have made
A ripple in the fabric, of time and space
A reaction to the decisions, that we've chosen to embrace

Like a stone cast into water, the effects will spread
A concentric circle, of consequences ahead
Some will be gentle whispers, while others will roar
A reflection of the power, that our choices hold in store

We reap what we have sown, in the fields of our past
A harvest of consequence, that will forever last
The seeds of our intentions, will sprout and grow
A garden of outcome, that our actions will bestow

But consequence is not punishment, nor is it fate
It's the natural unfolding, of the choices we create
A mirror held to our souls, reflecting what we've done
A chance to learn and grow, from the consequences we've begun

So let us choose with wisdom, and hearts that are true
For the consequences of our actions, will shape the world anew
And though we cannot see, the fullness of what's to come
We can trust that consequence will be the fruit of what we've become.

The Warmth

The warmth of love, it spreads like fire
Melting fears, and soothing desire
A gentle heat, that seeps into the bone
A comforting presence, that's always known

It's the touch of a hand, on a winter's night
A reassuring whisper, that everything's alright
A soft blanket of kindness, that wraps around the heart
A sense of belonging, that never departs

The warmth of memories, it lingers on
A bittersweet nostalgia, that's never gone
A faded photograph, of laughter and of tears
A treasured recollection, of joyous years

It's the smell of freshly baked bread
A warm invitation, to a loving home instead
A crackling fireplace, on a cold winter's day
A cozy sanctuary, where love finds its way

The warmth of connection, it bridges the space
A heartfelt understanding, that time and distance can't erase
A deep and abiding friendship, that stands the test
A love that's strong and steadfast, and forever at its best

So let us cherish the warmth, that we share with glee
A precious gift of love, that's meant to be.

Stellar

In the velvet expanse of night's dark shade
A twinkling tapestry, of stars is displayed
Like diamonds on the cloth, of heaven's majestic throne
A stellar showcase, of celestial beauty shown

The moon, a glowing crescent, casts its silvery light
A beacon in the darkness, that guides us through the night
The stars, like ancient whispers, share their secrets with the wind
A cosmic language, that only the heart can comprehend

In the stellar vastness, we find our place
A tiny yet essential, thread in the cosmic lace
A dance of planets, spinning to the rhythm of the spheres
A symphony of wonder, that echoes through the years

Like stardust, we are born, of celestial fire and might
Our spirits infused with magic, on this stellar journey through the night
We shine like stars, with our own unique light
A constellation of dreams, that guide us through the dark of night

So let us marvel at the stellar sea
A celestial wonderland, that's meant to be
A reminder of the magic, that lies beyond our sight
A stellar tapestry, woven with love and light.